I0087430

A CourseGuide for

Basics of
Biblical
Aramaic

Miles V. Van Pelt

ZONDERVAN
ACADEMIC

ZONDERVAN ACADEMIC

A CourseGuide for Basics of Biblical Aramaic
Copyright © 2019 by Zondervan

Requests for information should be addressed to:
Zondervan, *3900 Sparks Dr. SE, Grand Rapids, Michigan 49546*

ISBN 978-0-310-11014-9 (softcover)

Printed in the United States of America

CONTENTS

Introduction 5

1. Alphabet 7

2. Vowels 10

3. Syllabification 13

4. Nouns: Absolute State 16

5. Nouns: Determined State 19

6. Nouns: Construct State 22

7. Conjunctions and Prepositions 25

8. Pronominal Suffixes 28

9. Pronouns.. 31

10. Adjectives and Numbers 34

11. Adverbs and Particles................................ 37

12. Introduction to Aramaic Verbs 40

13. Peal Perfect 43

14. Peal Imperfect 46

15. Peal Imperative 49

16. Peal Infinitive Construct............................ 52

17. Peal Participle 55

18. The Peil, Hithpeel, and Ithpeel Stems 58

19. The Pael Stem 60

20. The Hithpaal and Ithpaal Stems 63

21. The Haphel Stem 65

22. The Aphel, Shaphel, and Hophal Stems 67

Introduction

Welcome to *A CourseGuide for Basics of Biblical Aramaic*. These guides were created for formal and informal students alike who want to engage deeper in biblical, theological, or ministry studies. We hope this guide will provide an opportunity for you to grow not only in your understanding, but also in your faith.

How to Use This Guide

This guide is meant to be used in conjunction with the book *Basics of Biblical Aramaic* and its corresponding videos, *Basics of Biblical Aramaic Video Lectures*. After you have read each chapter in the book and watched the accompanying video lesson, the materials in this guide will help you review and assess what you have learned. Application-oriented questions are included as well.

Each CourseGuide has been individually designed to best equip you in your studies, but in general, you can expect the following components. Most CourseGuides begin every chapter with a "You Should Know" section, which highlights key terminology, people, and facts to remember. This section serves as a helpful summary for directing your studies. Reflection questions, typically two to three per chapter, prompt you to summarize key points you've learned. Discussion questions invite you to an even deeper level of engagement. Finally, most chapters will end with a short quiz to test your retention. You can find the answer key to each quiz at the bottom of the page following it.

For Further Study

CourseGuides accompany books and videos from some of the world's top biblical and theological scholars. They may be used independently, or in small groups or classrooms, offering quality instruction to equip students for academic and ministry pursuits. If you would like to engage in further study with Zondervan's CourseGuides, the full lineup may be viewed online. After completing your studies with *A CourseGuide for Basics of Biblical Aramaic*, we recommend moving on to *A CourseGuide for Basics of Biblical Hebrew* and *A CourseGuide for Hebrew for the Rest of Us*.

Alphabet

You Should Know

- Consonantal variance: dialectical differences
  - Hebrew ז may be replaced with ד in Aramaic.
  - Hebrew צ may be replaced with ט or ע in Aramaic.
  - Hebrew שׁ may be replaced with ת in Aramaic.
- Consonantal variance: interchangeable consonants
  - In Aramaic א and ה are interchangeable.
  - In Aramaic שׂ and ס are interchangeable.
- Words occurring under 70 times in Hebrew:
  - גְּבַר = man (H. 66 A. 21)
  - דִּין = judgment, justice (H. 20 A. 5)
  - דָּת = law, command, decree (H. 22 A. 14)
  - כְּתָב = writing, inscription, document (H. 17 A. 12)
  - מְדִינָה = province, city (H. 53 A. 11)
  - מִלָּה = word, matter, affair (H. 38 A. 24)
  - סָפַר = scribe (H. 53 A. 6)
  - צֶלֶם = statue, image (H. 15 A. 17)
  - שְׁאָר = rest, remains, remainder, remnant (H. 27 A. 12)
- Words occurring over 70 times in Hebrew:
  - אָב = father, ancestor (H. 1,221 A. 9)
  - בַּיִת = house, temple (H. 2,046 A. 44)
  - הֵיכָל = palace, temple (H. 80 A. 13)

- חַיִל = strength, army (H. 245 A. 7)
- חָכְמָה = wisdom (H. 149 A. 8)
- יוֹם = day (H. 2,303 A. 16)
- כָּהֵן = priest (H. 750 A. 8)
- מֶלֶךְ = king (H. 2,530 A. 180)
- נְבִיא = prophet (H. 317 A. 8)
- עֶבֶד = servant, slave (H. 803 A. 8)
- עַם = people, nation (H. 1,868 A. 15)
- רוּחַ = wind, spirit, mind (H. 378 A. 11)
- שֵׁם = name (H. 864 A. 12)
- שָׁנָה = year (H. 879 A. 7)

Quiz

1. (T/F) The Aramaic alphabet is identical to the Hebrew alphabet.

2. There are ___ letters in the Aramaic alphabet.
    a) 22
    b) 23
    c) 24
    d) 25

3. (T/F) The five letters that have final forms are צ ,פ ,נ ,מ ,כ.

4. (T/F) The six letters that may take the Daghesh Lene are ט ,פ ,כ ,ד ,ג ,ב.

5. The presence of the Daghesh Lene means you pronounce the letter:
    a) Soft
    b) Hard
    c) Twice
    d) Like a guttural

6. (T/F) A Daghesh Lene will only appear in a *begadkephat* letter.

7. ___ is the only semi-guttural.
    a) א
    b) ע

c) ר
d) י

8. (T/F) Gutturals reject Daghesh Forte.

9. Select the <u>incorrect</u> consonantal variation (dialectical difference).

a) ז and ד
b) ה and א
c) ת and שׁ
d) צ and ט

10. Select the <u>correct</u> consonantal variation (interchangeable consonants).

a) ה and א
b) א and ע
c) כ and ח
d) ר and ד

CHAPTER 2

Vowels

You Should Know

- Vocalization changes from Hebrew:
  - Hateph vowels may appear under non-gutturals.
  - Quiescent א may drop out.
  - Canaanite shift: The Hebrew Holem or Holem Waw may appear as Qamets.
  - Nasalization: The נ may be added to a word (often when a consonant in Hebrew would have been doubled).

- אֱנָשׁ = man, mankind, person, (collective) people [Canaanite shift (CS): Hebrew אֱנוֹשׁ]

- אָע = wood, tree, beam [consonantal variation (CV): ע < צ—Hebrew עֵץ]

- אֲרַע = earth, land (also spelled אֲרַק) [CV: ע < צ—Hebrew אֶרֶץ]

- בַּר = son; (mp construct) בְּנֵי

- בַּר = field, countryside

- דְּהַב = gold [CV: ד < ז—Hebrew זָהָב]

- דָּר = generation [CS: Hebrew דּוֹר]

- לִשָּׁן = tongue, language [CS: Hebrew לָשׁוֹן]

- מַנְדַּע = understanding [nasalization: Hebrew מַדָּע]

- פַּרְזֶל = iron [ב < פ]

- קָל = voice, sound [CS: Hebrew קוֹל]

- שׁוּר = wall
- תּוֹר = ox, bull [CV: ת < שׁ—Hebrew שׁוֹר]

Quiz

1. Which vowel is NOT a long vowel?

    a) בֵ

    b) בָ

    c) ב

    d) בֶ

2. (T/F) The reduced vowels appear only in the a, e, and i-classes.

3. Which type of vowel letter only appears at the end of a word?

    a) ה

    b) ו

    c) י

    d) None of the above

4. The Furtive Pathach only occurs under:

    a) ה and ח

    b) ח and ע

    c) ע and א

    d) ה and א

5. (T/F) Like in Hebrew, Hateph vowels are primarily restricted to gutturals in Aramaic.

6. Which of the following is NOT a proper vowel letter?

    a) בָּה

    b) בֶּה

    c) בֵּה

    d) בה

7. (T/F) Like the Hateph vowels, Shewa counts as a reduced vowel.

8. (T/F) The only vowel type that contains all five classes of vowels is short.

9. (T/F) Both לְמֵמַר and לְמֵאמַר appear in Aramaic and have the same meaning.

10. Explain the change between מַנְדַּע and מַדַּע.

   a) Nasalization
   b) Canaanite shift
   c) Addition of preposition מִן
   d) One of them is a Participle.

CHAPTER 3

Syllabification

You Should Know

- אַרְתַּחְשַׁשְׂתְּא = The highlighted Shewa is silent.

- אַרְתַּחְשַׁשְׂתְּא = The highlighted Daghesh is Lene.

- תִּתְּנֵי = The highlighted Daghesh is Forte.

- בָּבֶל = Babylon

- שְׁתַר בּוֹזְנַי = Shethar Bozenai

- עֲבֵד נְגוֹ = Abed Nego

- פָּרָס = Persia

- רְחוּם = Rehum

- שִׁמְשַׁי = Shimshai

- תַּתְּנַי = Tatnai

Quiz

1. There are only two types of syllables:
   a) Open and closed
   b) Pretonic and tonic
   c) Penultima and ultima
   d) Stressed and unstressed

2. (T/F) The majority of words in Aramaic are accented on the longer syllable.

3. (T/F) In the word אָמָּה there are two syllables: the first is open and the second is closed.

4. In the word נְבוּאָה there are three syllables. Select the correct syllable classification for each (remember the word is read right to left):

 a) Post-tonic, pretonic, and tonic
 b) Pretonic, pretonic, tonic
 c) Pretonic, tonic, post-tonic
 d) Propretonic, pretonic, tonic

5. When a Daghesh Forte is in a consonant, it _____ the sound of the letter.

 a) Hardens
 b) Softens
 c) Doubles
 d) Does not change

6. (T/F) A Shewa is silent if it is immediately preceded by a long vowel. In every other instance, it is vocal.

7. Given the first rule of Shewa, identify the correct change:

 a) לְשְׁמַיָּא becomes לִשְׁמַיָּא
 b) לְשְׁמַיָּא becomes לְשִׁמַיָּא
 c) לְשְׁמַיָּא becomes לָאשְׁמַיָּא
 d) לְשְׁמַיָּא becomes לְשְׁמַיָּא

8. Given the second rule of Shewa, identify the correct change:

 a) לְאֱלָה becomes לָאֱלָה
 b) לְאֱלָה becomes לֶאֱלָה
 c) לְאֱלָה becomes לְאֱלָה
 d) לְאֱלָה becomes לָאֱלָה

9. Identify the word with the Daghesh Forte:

 a) לְאֱלָה
 b) פְּרַס
 c) מַלְכָּא
 d) צִפַּר

10. Select the correct syllabification for אֲרַתְּחֲשַׁשְׂתָּא:

    a) אֲרוֹתַּחְוֹשַׁשְׂוֹתָא

    b) אוֹרוּתַּחְוֹשַׁשְׂוֹתָא

    c) אֲרוֹתַּחְוֹשַׁשְׂוֹתָא

    d) אֲרוֹתַּחְוֹשַׁשְׂוֹתָאו

CHAPTER 4

Nouns: Absolute State

You Should Know

- The noun מֶלֶךְ is made abstract by adding וּ to the back, thus מַלְכוּ.
- אַתּוּן = furnace (10x)
- גֹּב = pit, den (also spelled גוֹב and גֵּב) (10x)
- גּוֹא = midst, middle (also spelled גוֹ) (13x)
- זְמָן = time, a fixed time, turn (11x)
- הֵיוָן = animal, beast (20x)
- חֲסַף = moulded clay, pottery, earthenware (9x)
- טְעֵם = understanding, command, decree, advice, report (30x)
- נוּר = fire (17x)
- עִדָּן = time, moment (13x)
- פְּשַׁר = interpretation (32x)
- שָׁלְטָן = dominion, powers (14x)
- רָז = secret, mystery (9x)

Quiz

1. Which noun is masculine singular?

   a) חֵיוָה
   b) מִלָּה
   c) זְמָן
   d) הַדָּמִין

2. Which noun is masculine plural?

    a) רָזִין

    b) פַּרְזֶל

    c) נִבְזְבָּה

    d) קַיְט

3. Which noun is feminine plural?

    a) אֶצְבְּעָן

    b) עָלְמִין

    c) נִיחֹחִין

    d) עֲטָא

4. Feminine singular nouns can end in:

    a) ָה

    b) ָה and ָא

    c) ָה and ֵה

    d) ָה and ָע

5. (T/F) Sometimes masculine plural nouns take feminine plural endings.

6. The ending of the word מַלְכוּ is an example of:

    a) A defective feminine plural noun

    b) A Hebrew-like ending

    c) An abstract noun

    d) A vocative ending

7. Parse the word אֻמִּין.

    a) Masculine singular absolute

    b) Masculine plural absolute

    c) Feminine singular absolute

    d) Feminine plural absolute

8. Parse the word חֶלְמִין.

    a) Masculine singular absolute

    b) Masculine plural absolute

    c) Feminine singular absolute

    d) Feminine plural absolute

9. Give the meaning of the word רְן.

    a) King
    b) Furnace
    c) Pit
    d) Secret

10. Give the meaning of the word חֲסַף.

    a) Time
    b) Fire
    c) Pottery
    d) Middle

CHAPTER 5

Nouns: Determined State

You Should Know

- FS nouns have a ָ preceding the article.
- FP nouns have a ָ preceding the article.
- אִילָן = tree (6x)
- אֻמָּה = nation (8x)
- אֱסָר = prohibition (7x)
- אֲתַר = place, location (5x)
- גְּשֵׁם = body (6x)
- הַמְנִיךְ = chain (6x)
- זִיו = radiance, brightness, countenance (6x)
- זְמָר = stringed musical instrument, musical instruments (4x)
- יְקָר = dignity, honor (7x)
- מָאן = vessel (7x)

Quiz

1. (T/F) The proper translation of the word חֵיוָתָא is "the animal."

2. Choose the word that correctly represents the masculine singular determined.

   a) הַמְנִיכָּא
   b) הַמְנִיכָא
   c) הַמְנִיכָה
   d) הַהַמְנִיךְ

3. Choose the word that correctly represents the feminine singular determined.

    a) חֵיוְתָא

    b) חֵיוָא

    c) חֵיוְהָא

    d) חֵיוְתָא

4. Parse the noun מִלָּה.

    a) Feminine singular absolute

    b) Feminine singular determined

    c) Masculine singular absolute

    d) Masculine singular determined

5. The word יְקָר is best translated:

    a) Dignity

    b) Sort

    c) Vessel

    d) Musical instrument

6. The word אֲתַר is best translated:

    a) Prohibition

    b) Place

    c) Chain

    d) Kind

7. The word אַמָּה is best translated:

    a) Cubit

    b) Chain

    c) Nation

    d) Brightness

8. The word גְּשֵׁם is best translated:

    a) Name

    b) Body

    c) Location

    d) Countenance

9. (T/F) The definite article is the only way to make a noun definite in Aramaic.

10. (T/F) While there is no indefinite article in Aramaic, the number one (חַד) can act as the indefinite article.

CHAPTER 6

Nouns: Construct State

You Should Know

- דִּי = that, which, who, what, of (347x)

- מְדוֹר = abode, dwelling (4x)

- מָרֵא = lord (6x)

- סוֹף = end (5x)

- עֲנַף = bough, branch (4x)

- פֻּם = entrance, opening, mouth (6x)

- פִּתְגָם = decree, answer, word (6x)

- רְבוּ = greatness (5x)

- רוּם = height, highest point (5x)

- רַעְיוֹן = thought (6x)

- שָׁלוּ = negligence (5x)

- שָׁעָה = moment, short time (5x)

Quiz

1. (T/F) The definiteness or indefiniteness of a construct chain is determined by the definiteness or indefiniteness of the absolute or final noun.

2. (T/F) In the phrase דְּהַב דִּי־מַלְכָּא, the word דְּהַב is translated definite due to the word מַלְכָּא.

3. Parse the noun חַכִּימֵי.

   a) Masculine plural absolute

   b) Masculine plural determined

   c) Masculine plural construct

   d) Feminine plural construct

4. Parse the noun מִלַּת.

   a) Feminine singular absolute

   b) Masculine singular construct

   c) Feminine plural construct

   d) Feminine singular construct

5. Parse the noun מְדִינַת.

   a) Feminine plural construct

   b) Feminine singular construct

   c) Masculine singular absolute

   d) Feminine singular absolute

6. Choose the proper translation of שְׁמֵהּ דִּי־אֱלָהָא.

   a) His name is God.

   b) There he is, God!

   c) A name of God

   d) The name of God

7. What is the lexical form of אֱלָהִי?

   a) אֱלֹהִים

   b) אֱלָהִין

   c) אֱלָהּ

   d) אֵלֶּה

8. Choose the proper translation of אַתּוּן נוּרָא.

   a) A furnace of fire

   b) Burning fire

   c) The burning furnace

   d) The furnace of fire

9. Choose the proper translation of חַכִּימֵי בָבֶל.

    a) The wisdom of Babylon
    b) The wise man of Babylon
    c) The wise men of Babylon
    d) Babylon's wise

10. What is the meaning of the word דִּי?

    a) Of
    b) Who
    c) That
    d) All of the above

CHAPTER 7

Conjunctions and Prepositions

You Should Know

- Two uses of the preposition לְ in Aramaic: object marker and circumlocution
- אַף = also (4x)
- בְּרַם = except what, yet, but, however (5x)
- הֵן = if, whether (16x)
- לָהֵן ^I = therefore (3x)
- לָהֵן ^{II} = except, but, yet (7x)
- בְּ = in, through, by means of, with, from (227x)
- כְּ = like, as, corresponding to, about (63x)
- לְ = to, fore, as, near (387x)
- מִן = from, out of, since (125x)
- עַד = up to, even to, until, during, within (35x)
- עַל = upon, about, over, above (113x)
- עִם = with, together with (22x)
- קֳדָם = before, in front of, in the presence of (46x)

Quiz

1. Which set below would result in the conjunction וְ being spelled as וּ?
   a) ב and מ
   b) Monosyllabic nouns

c) Long vowels
d) ,ְ פ, מ, and ב

2. Prefix the conjunction וְ to the noun אֱנָשׁ.

a) וֱאֱנָשׁ
b) וֵאנָשׁ
c) וֵאֱנָשׁ
d) וֶאֱנָשׁ

3. Prefix the conjunction וְ to the noun יְקָר.

a) וִיְקָר
b) וַיְקָר
c) וִיקָר
d) וּיְקָר

4. (T/F) When the preposition לְ is used to mark the verbal object, you do not translate it.

5. Prefix the preposition בְּ to the noun שְׁמַיָּא.

a) בַּשְׁמַיָּא
b) בְּשׁמַיָּא
c) בִּשְׁמַיָּא
d) בִשְׁמַיָּא

6. Which of the following is NOT a proper spelling of the preposition מִן?

a) מִן־טַעַם
b) מֵאַרְעָא
c) מִבְּנֵי
d) מִנְחַבְרָתַהּ

7. Which of the following is NOT a conjunction?

a) אַף
b) הֵן
c) קֳדָם
d) לָהֵן

8. Which is NOT an acceptable translation of בִּשְׁמַיָּא וּבְאַרְעָא?

a) In the heavens and on the earth
b) Through the heavens and from the earth

c) By the heavens and by the earth
d) From the heavens and near the earth

9. Which is NOT an appropriate translation of עַד?

a) Up to
b) Until
c) Within
d) Over

10. (T/F) The conjunction לָכֵן may be translated as either "therefore" or "but."

CHAPTER 8

Pronominal Suffixes

You Should Know

- אֲחַשְׁדַּרְפַּן = satrap (9x)
- אָשַׁף = enchanter, sorcerer (6x)
- בְּעֵל־טְעֵם = lord, owner (3x)
- הַדָּבַר = high-ranking official, counselor (4x)
- חַרְטֹם = magician (5x)
- כְּנָת = associate, colleague; (mp) כְּנָוָת (7x)
- סְגַן = prefect, governor, official (5x)
- סָרַךְ = high official, commissioner, administrator (5x)
- רַבְרְבָן = lord, noble (9x)
- שָׂב = elder (5x)
- מַשְׁרוֹקִי = pipe, musical instrument (3x)
- סוּמְפֹּנְיָה = pipe, bagpipe, double-barreled flute (1x)
- פְּסַנְטֵרִין = stringed instrument, harp (1x)
- קִיתְרֹוס = lyre, zither, musical instruments (also spelled קַתְרֹוס) (1x)
- שַׂבְּכָא = stringed musical instrument; trigon, harp (also spelled סַבְּכָא) (3x)

Quiz

1. (T/F) In general, type 2 pronominal suffixes appear on singular nouns.

2. (T/F) You would never translate לְכֹם "to your."

3. (T/F) The 2fs and 2fp pronominal suffixes do not appear in the biblical Aramaic text.

4. What is the person, gender, and number of the suffix on עֲלוֹהִי?

   a) 1cs
   b) 3fs
   c) 3ms
   d) 3mp

5. (T/F) When a pronominal suffix is on a preposition, it should be translated as its object.

6. What is the person, gender, and number of the suffix on לַהּ?

   a) 3fs
   b) 3ms
   c) 1cp
   d) 3fp

7. What is the person, gender, and number of the suffix on לְהוֹן?

   a) 3ms
   b) 3mp
   c) 3fp
   d) 2mp

8. Parse the noun מַלְכוּתִי.

   a) Feminine plural with 1cs suffix
   b) Feminine singular with 1cs suffix
   c) Masculine singular with 1cs suffix
   d) Masculine plural with 3ms suffix

9. What is the meaning of the noun שָׂב?

   a) Lord
   b) Noble
   c) Elder
   d) Counselor

10. What is the meaning of the noun שָׁלוּ?

   a) Moment
   b) Kingdom
   c) Negligence
   d) Petition

CHAPTER 9

Pronouns

You Should Know

- Four uses of the independent personal pronoun: subject, copula, object, demonstrative pronoun

- Uses of the particle דִּי thus far: construct chain, relative pronoun, subordinating conjunction

- אֲנָה = I

- אֲנַ֫חְנָה = we

- אַנְתְּ/אַנְתָּה = you

- הוּא = he, it

- הִיא = she, it

- הִמּוֹ/הִמּוֹן/אִנּוּן = they

- דְּנָה = this (ms)

- דָּא = this (fs)

- מָה = what?; לְמָה = why?; כְּמָה = how?; מָה דִי = whatever

- מַן = who?; מַן דִּי = whoever

- כִּדְנָה = thus

- כָּל־קֳבֵל דְּנָה = therefore, because of this, for this reason

- עַל־דְּנָה = therefore, on account of this, concerning this

Quiz

1. Which use of the pronoun is demonstrated by the phrase
וְהִיא תְּקוּם לְעָלְמַיָּא?
   a) Subject
   b) Copula
   c) Object
   d) Demonstrative pronoun

2. Which use of the pronoun is demonstrated by the phrase
הוּא צַלְמָא רֵאשֵׁהּ דִּי־דְהַב?
   a) Subject
   b) Copula
   c) Object
   d) Demonstrative pronoun

3. Which use of the pronoun is demonstrated by the phrase
מַן־אִנּוּן שְׁמָהָת גֻּבְרַיָּא?
   a) Subject
   b) Copula
   c) Object
   d) Demonstrative Pronoun

4. (T/F) When a demonstrative is modifying a noun, such as
בְּקַרְנָא־דָא, you do not translate the definite article on קֶרֶן "horn."

5. What is the best translation of כִּדְנָה?
   a) Thus
   b) Like this
   c) Like him
   d) According to this

6. What is the best translation of the phrase כָּל־קֳבֵל דְּנָה?
   a) Concerning this
   b) All because of this
   c) All on account of this
   d) For this reason

7. What is the best translation of the phrase עַל־דְּנָה?

   a) Over this
   b) Above it
   c) Therefore
   d) Thus

8. (T/F) When דִּי appears after an interrogative pronoun, the pronoun becomes indefinite (-ever).

9. Which of the following is NOT a form of the 3mp pronoun "they"?

   a) הִמּוֹ
   b) אִנִּין
   c) הִמּוֹן
   d) אִנּוּן

10. Which of the following is NOT a near demonstrative pronoun?

   a) אִלֵּין
   b) דָּא
   c) אֵלֶּה
   d) אֵלֶּךְ

CHAPTER 10

Adjectives and Numbers

You Should Know

- Attributive adjecties agree with the noun they modify in gender, number, and state.

- Predicative adjectives agree with the noun they modify in gender and number, and they are always in the absolute state.

- Substantive adjectives act like a noun and do not modify a noun.

- The two types of numbers are ordinals (1st, 2nd, etc.) and cardinals (1, 2, 3, etc.).

- אָחֳרָן = other, another (11x)

- חַי = living, alive, (noun) life (7x)

- יַצִּיב = certain, true, reliable, exact (5x)

- יַתִּיר = extraordinary; (adverb) exceedingly (8x)

- עִלָּי = superior, highest, the most-high (18x)

- עֶלְיוֹן = the Most High (4x)

- קַדִּישׁ = holy (13x)

- רַב = great (23x)

- שַׂגִּיא = great, much, many; (adverb) very much (13x)

- שַׁלִּיט = powerful, mighty (10x)

- תַּקִּיף = strong, mighty (5x)

Quiz

1. If an adjective agrees with the noun it modifies in gender and number and is in the absolute state, then it is in the _____ position.
   a) Attributive
   b) Predicative
   c) Substantive
   d) Adverbial

2. If an adjective agrees with the noun it modifies in gender, number, and state, then it is in the _____ position.
   a) Attributive
   b) Predicative
   c) Substantive
   d) Adverbial

3. The phrase כָּל־מֶלֶךְ רַב וְשַׁלִּיט is an example of the _____ use of the adjective.
   a) Attributive
   b) Predicative
   c) Substantive
   d) Adverbial

4. The phrase קַדִּישֵׁי עֶלְיוֹנִין is an example of the _____ use of the adjective.
   a) Attributive
   b) Predicative
   c) Substantive
   d) Adverbial

5. What is the best English translation of the phrase מְאָה וְעֶשְׂרִין?
   a) One hundred and twenty
   b) Twenty hundred
   c) One hundred and ten
   d) One hundred plus twenty

6. What is the best English translation of the phrase שִׁתִּין וְתַרְתֵּין?
   a) Twenty-six
   b) Sixty-two

c) Sixty plus twenty
d) Two years

7. In the phrase וּמַלְכוּ רְבִיעָיָה תֶּהֱוֵא תַקִּיפָה כְּפַרְזְלָא, which word is תַקִּיפָה modifying?

a) כְּפַרְזְלָא
b) וּמַלְכוּ
c) רְבִיעָיָה
d) תֶּהֱוֵא

8. What is the meaning of the word יַתִּיר?

a) Exceedingly
b) Rest
c) Great
d) Powerful

9. What is the meaning of the word שַׂגִּיא?

a) Strong
b) Other
c) Holy
d) Much

10. What is the meaning of the word סְגַן?

a) Elder
b) Governor
c) Great
d) Closed

CHAPTER 11

Adverbs and Particles

You Should Know

- אֱדַיִן = then (also בֵּאדַיִן) (57x)

- אָסְפַּרְנָא = completely, exactly, diligently (7x)

- כֵּן = thus, so (8x)

- כְּנֵמָא = thus, so (5x)

- כְּעַן = now (13x)

- כְּעֶנֶת = now (always at the end of a phrase) (4x)

- תַּמָּה = there (4x)

- אַל = no, not (4x)

- אִיתַי = there is, are (19x)

- הֲ = interrogative, particle (7x)

- לָא = no, not (82x)

- אֲלוּ = look! Behold! (5x)

- אֲרוּ = look! Behold! (5x)

Quiz

1. (T/F) You should translate the words אֱדַיִן and בֵּאדַיִן differently due the to the addition of the preposition.

2. (T/F) The accusative particle in Aramaic only appears twice.

3. What is the meaning of תַּמָּה?

    a) Then

    b) Thus

    c) There

    d) Three

4. What is the meaning of אִיתַי?

    a) Behold

    b) There is

    c) There is not

    d) Thus

5. What is the meaning of כְּעֶנֶת?

    a) Then

    b) Now

    c) So

    d) No

6. What is the meaning of יַצִּיב?

    a) Reliable

    b) Great

    c) Now

    d) Strong

7. What is the meaning of עִם?

    a) People

    b) With

    c) If

    d) On

8. Parse the word שַׂגִּיא.

    a) Feminine singular determined

    b) Masculine singular determined

    c) Masculine singular absolute

    d) Feminine singular absolute

9. Parse the word שָׁלְטָן.

    a) Masculine singular absolute

    b) Masculine plural absolute

c) Feminine plural absolute
d) Feminine singular absolute

10. (T/F) The word יְתִירָא could be either masculine singular definite or feminine singular absolute.

CHAPTER 12

Introduction to Aramaic Verbs

You Should Know

- Peal stem = voice: active; action: simple
- Pael stem = voice: active; action: intensive/causative
- Peil stem = voice: passive; action: simple
- Hithpeel stem = voice: reflexive/passive; action: simple
- Hithpaal stem = voice: reflexive/passive; action: intensive
- Haphel stem = voice: active; action: causative
- Hophal stem = voice: passive; action: causative
- הוה = (Peal) to be, happen, exist (71x)
- יתב = (Peal) to sit, dwell, reside; (Haphel) to allow to dwell (5x)
- תוב = (Peal) to return, come back; (Haphel) to give back, bring back (8x)
- עבד = (Peal) to do, make; (Hithpeel) to be made, be performed (28x)
- שכח = (Hithpeel) to be found; (Haphel) to get (18x)

Quiz

1. The stem determines what about a verb?
   a) Its basic meaning
   b) Its mood and voice

    c) Its mood and action

    d) Its voice and action

2. (T/F) Both Hebrew and Aramaic have seven core stems.

	Simple	Intensive	Causative
Active	1	2	3
Passive	4	5	6
Reflexive/Passive	7	8	9

3. Using the diagram above, identify where the Peal stem belongs.

    a) 1 and 2

    b) 1

    c) 4

    d) 1 and 4

4. Using the diagram above, which stem belongs in the place of 7?

    a) Niphal

    b) Hithpaal

    c) Hithpeel

    d) Peil

5. What is the base stem in Aramaic?

    a) Qal

    b) Peal

    c) Peil

    d) Piel

6. (T/F) Aramaic lacks the Infinitive Absolute conjugation of Hebrew.

7. Which conjugation will have no person, gender, or number (PGN) when parsing?

    a) Perfect

    b) Participle

    c) Infinitive Construct

    d) All conjugations have PGN

8. What is the meaning of the verb עבד?

   a) To work
   b) To serve
   c) To do
   d) To fix

9. What is the meaning of the verb שכח?

   a) To be found
   b) To find
   c) To forget
   d) To remember

10. What is the meaning of the verb אבד?

    a) To eat
    b) To work
    c) To make
    d) To perish

CHAPTER 13

Peal Perfect

You Should Know

- The Peal stem corresponds to the Hebrew Qal.

- Peal stem = voice: active; action: simple

- In the Perfect biconsonantal verbs, the vowel letter appears as a Qamets.

- In the Perfect geminate, verbs have only one geminate consonant and sometimes no Daghesh.

- In III-ה/III-א verbs, the א/ה may become ו, י, or drop off.

- אתה = (Peal) to come; (Haphel) to bring; (Hophal) to be brought (21x)

- בעא = (Peal) to seek, request; to be about to; (Pael) to call upon, search eagerly (12x)

- דור = (Peal) to live, dwell (13x)

- חוה = (Pael) to show, make known; (Haphel) to make known, interpret (15x)

- יהב = (Peal) to give; (Hithpeel) to be given (28x)

- נפק = (Peal) to go out; come forth, be issued; (Haphel) to take out (12x)

- סגד = (Peal) to pay homage, bow down in worship (12x)

- עלל = (Peal) to go in, enter; (Haphel) to bring in; (Hophal) to be brought (17x)

- רמה = (Peal) to throw, place, impose; (Hithpeel) to be thrown (12x)

- שנה = (Peal) to be different, be changed; (Pael) to change, violate an order; (Ithpaal) to be changed; (Haphel) to alter, violate (22x)

Quiz

1. What type of action is communicated by the Perfect conjugation?
   a) Simple
   b) Continuous
   c) Complete
   d) Past

2. (T/F) In Aramaic the stem vowel for the Peal Perfect may alternatively appear as a Hireq or a Tsere.

3. Select the 2ms form of the verb כתב.
   a) כְּתַבְתָּ
   b) כְּתְבַת
   c) כְּתַבְתּוּן
   d) כְּתְבְתְ

4. Select the 1cs form of the verb כתב.
   a) כְּתְבַת
   b) כְּתְבַתִי
   c) כְּתַבִי
   d) כְּתַבְתִי

5. Select the 2mp form of the verb כתב.
   a) כְּתֹבוּ
   b) כְּתַבְתּוּן
   c) כְּתַבְתּוּ
   d) כְּתַבְתֶּם

6. Select the correct PGN for the verb עַל.
   a) 2ms
   b) 3fs

    c) 3ms

    d) 1cs

7. Select the correct PGN for the verb שָׂמֵת.

    a) 3fs

    b) 2ms

    c) 3ms

    d) 1cs

8. Determine the lexical form of the verb בְּעָה.

    a) בעה

    b) בעא

    c) בוא

    d) בְעע

9. Determine the lexical form of the verb קָם.

    a) קום

    b) קים

    c) קמה

    d) קמם

10. Determine the lexical form of the verb עֲלַת.

    a) עול

    b) עלה

    c) עלא

    d) עלל

ANSWER KEY

1. c, 2. T, 3. d, 4. a, 5. b, 6. c, 7. d, 8. b, 9. a, 10. d

CHAPTER 14

Peal Imperfect

You Should Know

- In the Imperfect, I-י verbs may become Hireq Yod (יֵיטַב) or fall out (יִתֵּב).

- In the verb יכל, the first root letter is variable between Hireq (Yod) and Shureq.

- The verb ידע replaces the י with a נ.

- The verb הלך is often spelled without the ל.

- בהל = (Pael) to frighten, terrify; (Hithpeel) to hasten; (Hithpaal) to be frightened, be terrified (11x)

- דקק = (Peal) to be crushed into small pieces, ground up fine; (Haphel) to crush (10x)

- יקד = (Peal) to burn (8x)

- כלל = (Shaphel) to finish; (Hishtaphel) to be finished (8x)

- מטא = (Peal) to reach to, attain to, come upon; to occur, happen (8x)

- סלק = (Peal) to go up, come up; (Haphel) to take up; (Hophal) to be lifted up (8x)

- עדה = (Peal) to pass away, take away, revoke, touch (9x)

- פלח = (Peal) to serve (10x)

- צבה = (Peal) to desire, wish for, like (10x)

- שפל = (Haphel) to humiliate, humble (4x)

Quiz

1. (T/F) The Peal Imperfect is primarily concerned with future actions.

2. Select the 3mp form of the verb כתב in the Peal Imperfect.

    a) יִכְתְּבוּ
    b) יִכְתַּב
    c) יִכְתְּבוּן
    d) יִכְתְּבוּן

3. Select the 1cs form of the verb כתב in the Peal Imperfect.

    a) אִכְתַּב
    b) אֶכְתַּב
    c) אֶכְתַּב
    d) אֶכְתַּב

4. Select the 3fp form of the verb כתב in the Peal Imperfect.

    a) יִכְתְּבָן
    b) יִכְתְּבָה
    c) תִּכְתְּבָן
    d) יִכְתְּבָן

5. What is the root of the verb יִתֵּב?

    a) נתב
    b) תבה
    c) תיב
    d) יתב

6. What is the root of the verb וִיהָךְ?

    a) יהך
    b) והך
    c) הלך
    d) נהך

7. What is the root of the verb יְקְרוֹן?

    a) יקר
    b) קרא
    c) קרה
    d) קיר

8. What is the meaning of the word סלק?

    a) To come up
    b) To pass away
    c) To cut
    d) To loosen

9. What is the meaning of the word פלח?

    a) To open
    b) To desire
    c) To burn
    d) To serve

10. What is the meaning of the verb שפל?

    a) To fall
    b) To humble
    c) To desire
    d) To serve

CHAPTER 15

Peal Imperative

You Should Know

- The Negative Imperative is formed with לָא or אַל plus the Imperfect.

- Generally, the Imperative uses the same stem vowel as the Imperfect.

- In the I-י and I-נ Imperative, the first root letter falls off.

- In the III-ה Imperative, the verb usually ends in י or ו and not ה or א.

- אזל = (Peal) to go, walk (7x)

- בטל = (Peal) to cease, be discontinued; (Pael) to stop, bring to an end (6x)

- בקר = (Pael) to seek, investigate; (Hithpaal) to be investigated (5x)

- גזר = (Peal) to cut, divine; (Hithpeel) to be broken off, break away from (6x)

- דחל = (Peal) to fear; (Pael) to startle (6x)

- זוע = (Peal) to tremble, shake (4x)

- חבל = (Pael) to hurt, destroy; (Hithpaal) to be destroyed, perish (6x)

- חלף = (Peal) to pass over (4x)

- טרד = (Peal) to drive away (4x)

- כהל = (Peal) to be able, be capable (4x)

Quiz

1. Select the 2mp form of the verb כתב in the Peal Imperative.

   a) כְּתֻבוּ
   b) כְּתֻבוּ
   c) כְּתֻבוּ
   d) כְּתֻבוּ

2. Select the 2fs form of the verb כתב in the Peal Imperative.

   a) כְּתֻבִי
   b) כְּתֻבִי
   c) כְּתֻבִי
   d) כְּתֻבִי

3. Parse the verb שְׁבֻקוּ.

   a) Peal Perfect 2mp
   b) Peal Perfect 3mp
   c) Peal Imperative 3mp
   d) Peal Imperative 2mp

4. Parse the verb פְּרֻק.

   a) Peal Perfect 3ms
   b) Peal Imperative 2ms
   c) Peal Infinitive Construct
   d) Peal Imperative 2fs

5. Parse the verb אֲמַרוּ.

   a) Peal Imperative 2mp
   b) Peal Imperative 3mp
   c) Peal Perfect 3mp
   d) Peal Perfect 3mp

6. Parse the verb אֱמַרוּ.

   a) Peal Perfect 3mp
   b) Peal Perfect 2mp
   c) Peal Imperative 2mp
   d) Peal Imperfect 3mp

7. Parse the verb חֱיִי.

   a) Peal Imperative 2fs
   b) Peal Imperative 2ms
   c) Peal Perfect 2fs
   d) Peal Perfect 3fs

8. Parse the verb בְּעָה.

   a) Peal Imperative 2ms
   b) Peal Imperative 2fs
   c) Peal Perfect 3fs
   d) Peal Perfect 3ms

9. Translate the clause מַלְכָּא לְעָלְמִין חֱיִי אֱמַר חֶלְמָא לְעַבְדָיךְ.

   a) The king lives forever! Let him speak the dream to your servants.
   b) Oh king, live forever! Speak the dream to his servants.
   c) Oh king, live forever! Speak the dream to your servant.
   d) Oh king, live forever! Speak the dream to your servants.

10. Translate the clause עַבְדּוֹהִי דִּי־אֱלָהָא עִלָּיָא פֻּקוּ וֶאֱתוֹ.

    a) Servant of the God Most High, come forth and come out!
    b) His servants of the God Most High, come forth and come out!
    c) Servants of the God Most High, come forth and come out!
    d) His servants, the God Most High, came forth and they came out.

CHAPTER 16

Peal Infinitive Construct

You Should Know

- The distinguishing diagnostic of the Peal Infinitive is the מְ (Mem Hireq) prefix (not a preposition).

- Purpose, Intention, Result: use of the Infinitive commonly translated with "in order to"

- Complementary: use of the Infinitive as a helping verb (such as with יכל)

- Temporal: use of the Infinitive used to communicate when an action took place

- Permission: use of the Infinitive with an Imperfect of the same verbal root (e.g. לְמִנְתַּן תִּנְתֵּן "you may give")

- כפת = (Peal) to be bound; (Pael) to bind (4x)

- מחא = (Peal) to strike; (Pael) to strike; (Hithpeel) to be impaled (4x)

- מלל = (Pael) to speak (17x)

- מנה = (Peal) to count; (Pael) to install, appoint (5x)

- נדב = (Hithpaal) to be agreeable, willing; to donate (3x)

- נזק = (Peal) to come to grief; (Haphel) to damage, suffer harm (3x)

- נחת = (Peal) to come down; (Haphel) to deposit (6x)

- ערב = (Pael) to mix; (Hithpaal) to mingle (4x)

- צבע = (Pael) to moisten, wet; (Hithpeel) to become moist, wet (5x)

- צלח = (Haphel) to cause someone to prosper, make progress (4x)

Quiz

1. (T/F) In the Peal stem, the Infinitive Construct may be distinguished by the presence of the preposition מִן on the front of the verb (i.e. מִכְתַּב).

2. (T/F) The א of I-א verbs in the Peal Infinitive Construct are quiescent and often fall off completely.

3. The verb הלך in Aramaic is unusual because:
   a) The ה acts like a I-י
   b) The ל doubles
   c) The ל falls off
   d) A נ is often added

4. Which use of the Infinitive Construct is used in the clause דִּי יְכֵלְתָּ לְמִגְלֵא רָזָה דְנָה?
   a) Purpose, Intention, Result
   b) Complementary
   c) Temporal
   d) Permission

5. Which use of the Infinitive Construct is used in the clause בִּשְׁאָר כַּסְפָּא וְדַהֲבָה לְמֶעְבַּד כִּרְעוּת אֱלָהֲכֹם תַּעַבְדוּן?
   a) Purpose, Intention, Result
   b) Complementary
   c) Temporal
   d) Permission

6. Which use of the Infinitive Construct is used in the clause בֵּאדַיִן קָמוּ זְרֻבָּבֶל בַּר־שְׁאַלְתִּיאֵל וְיֵשׁוּעַ בַּר־יוֹצָדָק וְשָׁרִיו לְמִבְנֵא בֵּית אֱלָהָא?
   a) Purpose, Intention, Result
   b) Complementary
   c) Temporal
   d) Permission

7. Which use of the Infinitive Construct is used in the clause וּשְׁאָר חַשְׁחוּת בֵּית אֱלָהָךְ דִּי יִפֶּל־לָךְ לְמִנְתַּן תִּנְתֵּן מִן־בֵּית גִּנְזֵי מַלְכָּא?
   a) Purpose, Intention, Result
   b) Complementary

   c) Temporal

   d) Permission

8. Which use of the Infinitive Construct is used in the phrase
וּכְמִקְרְבֵהּ לְגֻבָּא לְדָנִיֵּאל בְּקָל עֲצִיב זְעִק?

   a) Purpose, Intention, Result

   b) Complementary

   c) Temporal

   d) Permission

9. (T/F) In Aramaic the pronominal suffix may serve as the object or the subject of the Infinitive Construct.

10. Select the form of the verb כתב in the Peal Infinitive Construct.

   a) מְכָתַּב

   b) לְכְתַּב

   c) מִכְתַּב

   d) כְתַּב

CHAPTER 17

Peal Participle

You Should Know

- The attributive use of the Participle (PTC) agrees with the noun it modifies in gender, number, and state.

- The predicative use of the Participle appears in the absolute state and agrees with the noun in gender and number.

- The substantive use of the Participle serves as a noun and does not modify a noun.

- A Participle with a Perfect or Imperfect form of הוה is translated like a finite verb (similar to the Greek periphrastic construction).

- With a regular (finite) verb, the Participle may be translated like a Perfect or Imperfect verb.

- A diagnostic feature of the Peal Participle is the Qamets Tsere.

- A diagnostic feature of the passive Peal Participle is the Hireq Yod stem vowel.

- קטל = (Peal) to kill; (Hithpeel) to be killed; (Pael) to kill; (Hithpaal) to be killed (7x)

- רשם = (Peal) to write, inscribe (7x)

- שבח = (Pael) to praise (5x)

- שבק = (Pael) to leave behind, leave alone; (Hithpeel) to be left, pass on (5x)

- שֵׁיזָב = (Shaphel) to rescue, save, deliver (9x)

- שְׁלֵט = (Peal) to rule over, to have power over, to make oneself master of; (Haphel) to make someone ruler (7x)

- שְׂרה = (Peal) to be(come) strong; to grow hard, become arrogant; (Pael) to become strong, enforce (6x)

Quiz

1. The Participle is a verbal:

    a) Participle
    b) Noun
    c) Adjective
    d) Form

2. (T/F) The active Peal Participle uses an irreducible Qamets under the first root letter, except in the propretonic position.

3. The passive Peal Participle replaces the Qamets under the first root letter with a Shewa and has what vowel after the second root letter?

    a) ָ
    b) ִי
    c) וֹ
    d) ִי

4. Which use of the Participle is used in the phrase וּמַן־דִּי־לָא יִפֵּל וְיִסְגֻּד יִתְרְמֵא לְגוֹא־אַתּוּן נוּרָא יָקֵדְתָּא?

    a) Attributive
    b) Predicative
    c) Substantive
    d) Periphrastic

5. Which use of the Participle is used in the phrase בְּרִיךְ אֱלָהֲהוֹן?

    a) Attributive
    b) Predicative
    c) Substantive
    d) Imperative

6. Parse the verb חֲזָה.

   a) Peal PTC ms
   b) Peal Perfect 3ms
   c) Peal Imperative 2ms
   d) Peal PTC fs

7. Parse the verb יָכֵל.

   a) Peal active PTC ms
   b) Peal passive PTC ms
   c) Peal Perfect 3ms
   d) Peal Imperfect 3ms

8. Parse the verb הֲוֵיתָ.

   a) Peal PTC fp
   b) Peal Perfect 3fs
   c) Peal Perfect 2fs
   d) Peal Perfect 2ms

9. Parse the verb נְפַק.

   a) Peal active PTC ms
   b) Peal active PTC ms
   c) Peal Perfect 3ms
   d) Peal Imperative

10. Identify the verbal root of קָאֵם.

    a) קים
    b) קאם
    c) קום
    d) קמה

CHAPTER 18

The Peil, Hithpeel, and Ithpeel Stems

You Should Know

- Peil stem = voice: passive; action: simple
- The Peil Perfect 3ms is identical to the Peal passive PTC ms.
- The Peil is equivalent to the Hebrew Niphal stem.
- Hithpeel stem = voice: reflexive/passive; action: simple
- Metathesis occurs when a ת switches places with a sibilant (שׁ, שׂ, ס, צ).
- A diagnostic feature of the Infinitive Construct in derived stems is Qamets He (הָ).
- A helping word for the Hithpeel Participle is "being" (e.g. מִתְבְּנֵא "being built").
- Ithpeel stem = voice: reflexive/passive; action: simple
- The Ithpeel stem differs from the Hithpeel in that the preformative הת is replaced by את.
- The Ithpeel stem occurs four times, all in the Imperfect.

Quiz

1. What is metathesis?
    - a) When a ת and a שׁ switch places
    - b) When a ת becomes a שׁ
    - c) When a ת and any sibilant (S sound) switch places
    - d) When a sibilant (S sound) is added to the preformative

2. (T/F) The Hithpeel and the Ithpeel are only different due to their preformatives.

3. Parse the verb שְׁלִיחַ in the phrase בֵּאדַיִן מִן־קֳדָמוֹהִי שְׁלִיחַ פַּסָּא דִי־יְדָא.
   a) Peal passive PTC ms
   b) Peil Perfect 3ms
   c) Peal passive PTC ms
   d) Peil Perfect 3fs

4. (T/F) The Aramaic Peil stem has roughly the same meaning as the Hebrew Piel.

5. (T/F) The passive use of the Hithpeel stem is far more common than the reflexive use.

6. The Infinitive Construct of the Hithpeel stem is marked by:
   a) מ preformative
   b) ה ָ sufformative
   c) הִת preformative
   d) Nothing

7. Select the diagnostic features of the Ithpeel Perfect.
   a) אִת
   b) הִת
   c) ה ָ sufformative
   d) אָת

8. Select the diagnostic features of the Hithpeel Imperfect.
   a) יִת
   b) הִת
   c) תִת
   d) יִשׁ

9. Select the strong verb diagnostic features of the passive Hithpeel Participle.
   a) הִת
   b) מִת
   c) מִתְ י
   d) מ

10. (T/F) The Hithpeel active and passive forms are identical.

CHAPTER 19

The Pael Stem

You Should Know

- Pael stem = voice: active; action: intensive/causative

- The diagnostic features of the Pael stem are the Shewa, Pathach vowel, and Daghesh Forte.

- The Pael stem is equivalent to the Hebrew Piel stem.

- Compensatory lengthening occurs with the gutturals א, ע, and ר.

- Virtual doubling occurs with the gutturals ה and ח.

- The diagnostic features of the Pael Imperative are the Pathach vowel and the Daghesh Forte (there is no preformative on an Imperative).

- The diagnostic features of the Pael Perfect are the Pathach vowel and the Daghesh Forte.

- The ה of the Infinitive Construct may alternate with א.

Quiz

1. The Pael stem expresses a _____ type of action.
    a) Intensive
    b) Intensive/causative
    c) Passive
    d) Reflexive

2. Select the form that represents the Pael Perfect diagnostics.

   a) כִּתֵּב

   b) כַּתֵּב

   c) כַּתֵּב

   d) כְּתֵב

3. (T/F) In conjugations with a preformative or prefix, the Pael diagnostics should be memorized as Shewa, Pathach, and Daghesh Forte.

4. Select the guttural that would NOT result in compensatory lengthening.

   a) ר

   b) ה

   c) א

   d) ע

5. Select the diagnostic form for the Pael Infinitive Construct.

   a) מְכַתָּב

   b) כַּתֵּב

   c) כַּתָּבָה

   d) מְכַתְּבָה

6. Select the diagnostic form for the Pael PTC.

   a) מְכַתַּב

   b) כַּתְּבָה

   c) כְּתֵב

   d) מְכְתַּב

7. Select the diagnostic form of the passive Peal PTC.

   a) מְכַתַּב

   b) כְּתִיב

   c) מִתְכְּתֵב

   d) כְּתַב

8. What is the meaning of the verb תקף?

   a) To strike

   b) To loosen

   c) To be (become) strong

   d) To praise

9. What is the meaning of the verb שְׁלֵט?

   a) To rescue

   b) To grow

   c) To dwell

   d) To rule over

10. Translate the phrase נְפַק לְקַטָּלָה לְחַכִּימֵי בָּבֶל.

   a) And he went out to kill the wise men of Babylon.

   b) He went out killing the wise men of Babylon.

   c) He went out to kill the wise man of Babylon.

   d) He went out to kill the wise men of Babylon.

CHAPTER 20

The Hithpaal and Ithpaal Stems

You Should Know

- Hithpaal stem = voice: reflexive/passive; action: intensive
- The most common use of the Hithpaal stem is passive.
- It addition to metathesis, when a ת switches places, it may become a ט.
- The Hithpaal shares diagnostic features with the Pael: Pathach vowel and Daghesh Forte.
- The Ithpaal occurs only in the Perfect (3x).
- In the Infinitive Construct, the הִ may become וּת before a suffix.

Quiz

1. (T/F) There is no change in meaning between the Hithpaal and Ithpaal stems.

2. The Hithpaal is the ___ counterpart to the ___ stem.
    a) Passive/reflexive, Piel
    b) Passive/reflexive, Peal
    c) Intensive, Pael
    d) Passive/reflexive, Pael

3. (T/F) The reflexive meaning of the Hithpaal is more common than the passive meaning.

4. Identify the root of the verb יִצְטַבַּע.
    a) טבע
    b) צבע

c) תבע

d) יבע

5. (T/F) Both the Ithpeel and the Ithpaal only appear in the Perfect conjugation.

6. Identify the diagnostic form of the Hithpaal Perfect.

a) הִתְכַּתַב

b) הִתְכַּתֵּב

c) יִתְכַּתֵּב

d) הִתְכַּתַב

7. What unique diagnostic feature of the Infinitive Construct is present in the Hithpeel, Pael, and Hithpaal stems?

a) Shewa, Pathach, Daghesh Forte

b) Daghesh Forte in the second root letter

c) Qamets He at the end

d) הִתְ at the beginning

8. Parse the verb אֶשְׁתַּנּוּ.

a) Pael Imperfect 1cs

b) Peal Imperfect 1cs

c) Ithpaal Perfect 2mp

d) Ithpaal Perfect 3mp

9. Identify the root of the verb אֶשְׁתַּנִּי.

a) תנן

b) תנה

c) שתן

d) שנה

10. Parse the verb יִשְׁתַּמְּעוּן.

a) Hithpeel Imperfect 3mp

b) Hithpaal Imperfect 2mp

c) Hithpeel Imperfect 2ms

d) Hithpaal Imperfect 3mp

CHAPTER 21

The Haphel Stem

You Should Know

- Haphel stem = voice: active; action: causative
- The Haphel stem is equivalent to the Hebrew Hiphil stem.
- The persistent diagnostic feature of the Haphel is the הַ prefix.
- I-י verbs in the Haphel become I-ו.
- ה/א may become י (e.g. אתה = הַיְתִי).
- Since ה/א may become י and י may become ו, ה/א may become ו (e.g. אבד = תְּהוֹבֵד).
- Geminate verbs may either double the first root letter or undergo nasalization.

Quiz

1. The Haphel stem is the _____ and _____ stem in Aramaic.
    a) Active, intensive
    b) Active, causative
    c) Passive, reflexive
    d) Passive, intensive

2. What is the primary strong verb diagnostic of the Haphel stem?
    a) ה
    b) הַ
    c) הָ
    d) הִי

3. (T/F) Even in weak verbs, the ה of the Haphel stem remains stable.

4. When a Haphel Infinitive Construct takes a pronominal suffix, the
הָ ending becomes:

   a) ַת

   b) וּת

   c) ָ

   d) וּת/ַת

5. Reconstruct the root of the verb הַיְתִי.

   a) יתה

   b) הית

   c) אתה

   d) אתי

6. Reconstruct the root of the verb הַנְעֵל.

   a) נעל

   b) עלל

   c) עיל

   d) עלה

7. (T/F) The Haphel verb הַדֵּקֶת is an example of gemination; it originally had two ד (now marked by the Daghesh Forte).

8. Haphel verbs that appear to begin with a ו were originally:

   a) I-י

   b) I-נ

   c) I-ה

   d) I-ו

9. Parse the verb הֵימֵן.

   a) Haphel Imperative 2ms

   b) Haphel Perfect 2ms

   c) Haphel Perfect 3ms

   d) Haphel Infinitive Construct

10. Parse the verb יְהָתִיבוּן.

   a) Haphel Perfect 3mp

   b) Haphel Imperfect 3cp

   c) Haphel Imperfect 2mp

   d) Haphel Imperfect 3mp

CHAPTER 22

The Aphel, Shaphel, and Hophal Stems

You Should Know

- Hophal stem = voice: passive; action: causative

- The Aphel and Shaphel stems are alternative forms of the Hophal stem.

- The diagnostic feature of the Aphel is א.

- In the Imperfect and Participle, the Aphel's א falls off.

- Once the Aphel's א falls off, the preformative vowel may be Pathach, Shewa, or Qamets.

- There are only three verbs that appear in the Shaphel: שׁיזב, שׁיציא, and כלל.

- The lexical forms of the verbs שׁיזב and שׁיציא include the שׁ preformative.

- The passive counterpart to the Haphel is Hophal.

- The Hophal only occurs in the Perfect conjugation.

- The preformative vowel of the Hophal is Qamets Hatuf or Qibbuts.

- I-א verbs in the Hophal become Tsere Yod (e.g. הֵיתָיוּ).

- The passive/reflexive counterparts to the Pael are Hithpaal and Ithpaal.

- The three causative active stems are Haphel, Aphel, and Shaphel.

- The three simple passive stems are Peil, Hithpeel, and Ithpeel.

Quiz

1. (T/F) The Aphel, Shaphel, and Hophal stems are alternative causative active stems.

2. (T/F) The Shaphel stem is a unique verbal stem that has a שׁ as the prefix, but it is not part of the verbal root.

3. (T/F) In the Shaphel verb שֵׁיזִיב, the שׁ is part of the lexical form.

4. (T/F) The Hophal stem is the passive counterpart to the Haphel stem.

5. Parse the verb אַתַּרוּ.

 a) Pael Imperfect 1cs
 b) Aphel Perfect 3mp
 c) Aphel Imperative 2mp
 d) Pael Imperative 2mp

6. The only change between the diagnostics of the Haphel and Hophal stems is:

 a) The doubling of the second root consonant
 b) The addition of י
 c) The weak verb diagnostics
 d) The vowel under the prefix

7. Select the diagnostic feature of the Hophal stem.

 a) הָ
 b) ה
 c) הָ/ה
 d) הַ/ה

8. Identify the diagnostic form of the Infinitive Construct in the Shaphel.

 a) מְשֵׁיזָבָה
 b) שֵׁיזִיב
 c) שֵׁיזָבָה
 d) שֵׁיזָבָה

9. Identify the diagnostic form of the Aphel Imperfect.

   a) יְכְתֵּב
   b) יַאכְתֵּב
   c) אַכְתֵּב
   d) יְכָתֵּב

10. Identify the diagnostic form of the Haphel Participle.

   a) מַכְתֵּב
   b) מְהַכְתֵּר
   c) מָכְתֵּב
   d) מְהַכְתֵּבָה

Notes

www.ingramcontent.com/pod-product-compliance
Lightning Source LLC
Chambersburg PA
CBHW010920040426
42445CB00017B/1929